Pebble® Plus
Bilingüe/Bilingual

Datos geniales sobre deportes/
Cool Sports Facts

Datos geniales sobre fútbol

Cool Soccer Facts

por/by Abby Czeskleba

Editora consultora/Consulting Editor:

Gail Saunders-Smith, PhD

Consultor/Consultant: Craig Coenen, PhD
Profesor Adjunto de Historia/Associate Professor of History
Mercer County Community College
West Windsor, New Jersey

CAPSTONE PRESS
a capstone imprint

Pebble Plus is published by Capstone Press,
1710 Roe Crest Drive, North Mankato, Minnesota 56003.
www.capstonepub.com

Library of Congress Cataloging-in-Publication Data
Czeskleba, Abby.
[Cool soccer facts. Spanish.]
Datos geniales sobre fútbol = Cool soccer facts / by Abby Czeskleba.
p. cm. — (Pebble plus bilingue/bilingual)
Includes index.
ISBN 978-1-4296-9216-8 (library binding)
ISBN 978-1-62065-339-5 (ebook PDF)
1. Soccer—Miscellanea—Juvenile literature. I. Title.
GV943.25.C94 2013
796.334—dc23   2011050106

Summary: Simple text and full-color photos illustrate facts about the rules, equipment, and records of soccer.

Editorial Credits
Erika L. Shores, editor; Strictly Spanish, translation services; Kyle Grenz, designer; Eric Manske, bilingual book designer
    and production specialist; Eric Gohl, media researcher

Photo Credits
AP Images, 15; Kevork Djansezian, 21; Tony Gutierrez, 19
Comstock Images, cover (soccer ball), back cover, 1
Dreamstime/Diademimages, 9
FIFA via Getty Images Inc./Joern Pollex, 7
Getty Images Inc./AFP/Matt Campbell, 11
MLS via Getty Images Inc./German Alegria, 17
Shutterstock/cjpdesigns, 5, 13; ostill, cover

Note to Parents and Teachers

The Datos geniales sobre deportes/Cool Sports Facts series supports national social studies
standards related to people, places, and culture. This book describes and illustrates soccer. The
images support early readers in understanding the text. The repetition of words and phrases
helps early readers learn new words. This book also introduces early readers to subject-specific
vocabulary words, which are defined in the Glossary section. Early readers may need assistance
to read some words and to use the Table of Contents, Glossary, Internet Sites, and Index
sections of the book.

Printed in the United States of America in North Mankato, Minnesota.
042013   007246R

Table of Contents

Tabla de contenidos

Goal!

In the United States,
it's called soccer. Nearly
everywhere else, fans call
it football. It's the world's
most popular sport.

¡Gol!

En Estados Unidos se llama soccer.
Casi en todos los demás lugares,
los aficionados lo llaman fútbol.
Es el deporte más popular
del mundo.

Cool Equipment

Adidas designs a new soccer ball
for each World Cup.
The World Cup is played
every four years.

Equipo genial

Adidas diseña un nuevo balón de
fútbol para cada Copa Mundial.
La Copa Mundial se juega
cada cuatro años.

Soccer players wear shoes
called cleats.
The shoes grip the field
when the players run.

Los jugadores de fútbol usan calzado
llamado zapatos con tapones o tacos.
El zapato se agarra al campo
cuando los jugadores corren.

Cool Rules

Referees try to stay away
from the soccer ball.
If the ball hits a referee,
play continues.

Reglas geniales

Los árbitros tratan de mantenerse
alejados del balón de fútbol.
Si el balón golpea a un árbitro,
la jugada continúa.

Players love to celebrate

scoring a goal.

But it's against the rules

to take off shirts to celebrate.

A los jugadores les encanta celebrar

cuando anotan un gol.

Pero es contra las reglas que se quiten

las camisetas para celebrar.

Cool Records

Pelé is a soccer legend.

He scored 1,281 goals in his career.

Pelé played on three World Cup championship teams.

Récords geniales

Pelé es una leyenda del fútbol.

Anotó 1,281 goles en su carrera.

Pelé jugó en tres equipos de campeonato de la Copa Mundial.

The Los Angeles Galaxy
played in front of 93,137 fans
in August 2009.
It was the biggest U.S. crowd
for a non-World Cup game.

El Galaxy de Los Ángeles jugó frente a
93,137 aficionados en agosto de 2009.
Fue la mayor multitud de Estados Unidos
para un partido que no fuera parte de
la Copa Mundial.

In 2002, Hakan Sükür
scored a goal in the first
11 seconds of a game.
It was the fastest goal
in World Cup history.

En 2002 Hakan Sükür anotó un
gol en los primeros 11 segundos
de un partido.
Es el gol más rápido de la
historia de la Copa Mundial.

Soccer star Mia Hamm scored
158 goals in world games.
She holds the record for
the most world game goals
by a male or female player.

La estrella de fútbol Mia Hamm anotó
158 goles en partidos mundiales.
Ella tiene el récord de más goles
en partidos mundiales de jugadores
varoniles o femeniles.

Glossary

career—the experiences an athlete has playing a sport over time

celebrate—to do something fun for a special occasion

legend—someone who is among the best in what they do

popular—liked or enjoyed by many people

record—when something is done better than anyone has ever done it before

World Cup—a soccer tournament held every four years; 32 teams from around the world compete to win the World Cup championship

Internet Sites

FactHound offers a safe, fun way to find Internet sites related to this book. All of the sites on FactHound have been researched by our staff.

Here's all you do:

Visit *www.facthound.com*

Type in this code: 9781429692168

Super-cool stuff! Check out projects, games and lots more at **www.capstonekids.com**

Glosario

la carrera—las experiencias que un atleta tiene al practicar un deporte a lo largo del tiempo

celebrar—hacer algo divertido para una ocasión especial

la Copa Mundial—un torneo de fútbol que se celebra cada 4 años; 32 equipos de todo el mundo compiten para ganar el campeonato de la Copa Mundial

la leyenda—alguien que está entre los mejores en lo que hace

popular—que le gusta a muchas personas

el récord—cuando alguien hace algo mejor de lo que lo han hecho antes los demás

Sitios de Internet

FactHound brinda una forma segura y divertida de encontrar sitios de Internet relacionados con este libro. Todos los sitios en FactHound han sido investigados por nuestro personal.

Esto es todo lo que tienes que hacer:

Visita *www.facthound.com*

Ingresa este código: 9781429692168

¡Algo súper divertido! Hay proyectos, juegos y mucho más en www.capstonekids.com

Index

Índice